THE BUSES OF
NORTHERN
SCOTTISH

PETER FINDLAY

AMBERLEY PUBLISHING

Acknowledgements

This book reflects my interest in the company, from childhood through to actually working with the company, covering the fleet from the early 1960s through to the late 1980s. Although the book title refers to Northern Scottish, it also covers the era of my childhood before the company was so renamed. The photos represent the vehicles I either saw, travelled on, drove, and or photographed. The same vehicle may appear twice, mainly to represent a livery change, or simply because I particularly liked that vehicle. The majority of photographs were taken by myself or acquired with copyright. I am indebted to James Mair and John Sinclair for allowing me to use some of their images to supplement my collection. Any copyright infringement reflects an age thing on my part rather than a deliberate attempt to breach anyone's copyright. I would like to express my appreciation to James Mair, Donald MacRae and Steven Pirie for their assistance in checking the accuracy of this book. I have to thank my dad, who not only gave me the interest in buses but also gave me the opportunity to develop my career in Public Transport. And finally a big thank you to my wife, Jean, who has over the years had to sit outside numerous bus depots, farms and scrapyards, long before the Kindle was invented.

First published 2013

Amberley Publishing
The Hill, Stroud
Gloucestershire, GL5 4EP

www.amberley-books.com

Copyright © Peter Findlay , 2013

The right of Peter Findlay
to be identified as the Author of this work
has been asserted in accordance with the
Copyrights, Designs and Patents Act 1988.

ISBN 978 1 4456 1528 8
E-BOOK 978 1 4456 1551 6

British Library Cataloguing in Publication Data.
A catalogue record for this book is available from the British Library.

Typeset in 9.5pt on 12pt Celeste.
Typesetting by Amberley Publishing.
Printed in the UK.

Northern Scottish

W. Alexander & Sons Ltd was formed during 1924. As an associate of the Scottish Motor Traction Company Ltd, it was the largest bus operating company in Scotland. Within the Alexander empire, operations had been split into three areas: Southern, Northern and Fife. In 1961 the Alexander business was formally split into three individual operating companies, each with their own headquarters and management teams. Although retaining the W. Alexander name, each company had a new trading name, and for the area between Dundee and Forres this was to be W. Alexander & Sons (Northern) Ltd. The other two operating areas were Fife and Midland. At the same time each company adopted a new livery for their respective fleets. Midland retained the traditional blue Alexander livery, Fife adopted a red livery, while the new Northern company adopted a striking yellow livery.

The Northern name was not, however, new to some areas as Alexander's had acquired the Elgin-based Scottish General (Northern) Omnibus Company in 1930, their vehicles carrying the Northern fleetname.

When formed in 1961, the Alexander Northern operation had depots at Dundee, Arbroath, Montrose, Forfar, Blairgowrie, Stonehaven, Aberdeen, Elgin, Buckie, Macduff, Huntly, Fyvie, Rosehearty and Peterhead. The company faced competition from a number of significant operators and between 1965 and 1967 the businesses of Strachan's of Ballater, Simpson's of Rosehearty and Forres, Burnett's of Mintlaw, and Mitchell's of Luthermuir were acquired, adding around seventy vehicles to the fleet. This also saw Northern acquiring depots in Forres, Mintlaw, Turriff and Ballater, plus a second Rosehearty depot. Outstations were also operated at Methlick, Tarland, Alford and similar rural outposts.

The bulk of operations from 1961 onwards were based on a network of rural bus services operating within the area of the local depot, with longer distance services linking the main towns and Aberdeen. The fleet inherited from the original Alexander company comprised mainly Leyland and AEC vehicles, with over fifty pre-war buses still in operational use. A small number of Bedford, Daimler and Albion vehicles were also allocated to Northern. Many of the inherited fleet would eventually receive the yellow livery, but most of the pre-war stock ran in blue until withdrawn from service within around two years. It would be 1962/63 before new deliveries arrived in yellow, these being mainly AEC Reliances. Due to the rural nature of the services operated, lightweight chassis vehicles were considered adequate and over the years large numbers of Albion Vikings and Fords would be the backbone of the fleet. Heavyweight Leyland Leopards would be acquired in small numbers for trunk services, as would the odd Bedford and Ford coach for hire and tour work.

The discovery of North Sea oil in the 1970s would see the Aberdeen area transform dramatically as Aberdeen became the hub of North Sea oil operations. While this brought benefits to the company such as the opportunity to operate a direct Aberdeen to London service, the availability of offshore work and the high wages available created employment difficulties for many companies and Northern would be no exception.

1985 would see a further restructure of Scottish Bus Group operations, with all subsidiary companies being renamed in corporate manner. For Alexander Northern, this meant adopting the Northern Scottish name. The depots at Montrose, Arbroath, Dundee and Blairgowrie were transferred to a new company, Strathtay Scottish.

The Scottish Bus Group SCOTMAP exercise would see significant changes to the network, with many routes curtailed or amended to reflect passenger usage. Although there was little competition on any of its rural service routes, competition on the longer distance routes came from a Perth-based company, Stagecoach. Management at the time thought it simply a matter of riding the storm as this upstart operator would quickly fold – how wrong they were! As the company headed towards privatisation the Northern Scottish name was dropped in favour of Bluebird Northern. This saw the reintroduction of the Bluebird emblem on some vehicles.

The end of the company came in March 1991 when it was sold to Stagecoach. The yellow livery was eventually phased out in favour of the standard Stagecoach livery, the new company operating under the name of Stagecoach Bluebird. The name and the livery live on however on a number of preserved vehicles.

Buses and Me!

How many of us grew up saying they wanted to be a bus driver? How many of us actually did it? Well, I can answer yes to both questions. So, what attracted me?

My father started driving buses for W. Alexander & Sons after demob, working from their Buckie depot, which at that time was based in Cluny Lane. At that point we stayed in Cullen and I can vaguely remember travelling from Cullen to Portgordon to visit my granny on a variety of buses ranging from pre-war TS7s to early AEC Reliances. Cullen Primary School was adjacent to the A98, therefore I could watch the buses pass by, and if I knew my father was on a particular shift I would always look to see what bus he had. I was often reprimanded by teachers for paying more attention to passing buses than to lessons. When father came home at night, he was always quizzed as to what buses he had driven that day. At an early age I knew there were PAs, As, ACs, PCs, etc., and although I knew they were all different I didn't really appreciate the different body and chassis types. I suppose this changed when I had to travel to Buckie High School by bus – I quickly realised that although there was an allocation of four Leyland Tiger PS1s at Buckie, and although they all looked pretty similar, there were slow ones and there were fast ones – and that applied to drivers as well … Occasionally something different would turn up – a Leyland Royal Tiger PC class certainly had the wow factor as you could sit at the front and watch the driver, while the NL class Albion Aberdonians had cold leather-style seats. Therefore the interest in buses and the desire to drive them started at an early age, but father always said there were better jobs and prospects to be had by working in an office or a bank. By the late 1960s he had been promoted to Inspector, then District Traffic Superintendent at Buckie, and the depot had relocated to a purpose-built unit on East Cathcart Street.

On leaving school at the age of 16, I started working in a bank – and hated every minute of it. With shoulder-length hair and platform shoes, the bank didn't really like me either, so I stuck it out for four years, and having not passed a single bank exam, we parted company. At the age of 20 my desire to drive buses was real – I knew my own mind and knew what I wanted to do, but still had a year to go before I was 21. I got a job in the office of the local bulb factory, and again because the office was at the front of the building, I could see the buses coming and going with factory workers. There were always rumours that the factory was going to close so I knew that there were no long-term career prospects and that suited me just fine. By this time my father realised I was serious about bus driving, but there was a father and son obstacle that was creating a problem – my long hair. I can still hear him today saying, 'There will be no long hair hippies driving my buses', and he was serious. I gave in, got my hair cut, and started my driving tuition. My father taught me, usually with buses from depots other than his own, and the first lesson was in a NMS registration AEC Reliance. I think father was quite surprised by how well I could handle a bus, but there was a reason for that and that is best left to speculation on the reader's part! The lessons continued, getting out in Fords and Albion Vikings. The test was applied for, taken with a 1956 HMS registration AEC Reliance, and I failed. The failure was a reverse manoeuvre that saw me clip the kerb, so intense reverse training was done before the resit, again in an AEC Reliance from the same batch, and this time I passed. What a great feeling that was – 21 years old and I could drive buses and coaches, and I had my red and white driver badge, number LL24026, and my green and white conductor badge, LL28409, to prove it. The only problem was that I didn't have a job, but at least my name was now on the waiting list. The fact that my licence was only single deck didn't bother me as Buckie had no deckers and Elgin only had two deckers, both Lowlanders, and deckers were being replaced with 53-seat Fords. That would change however – more about this later on. To this day, though, it annoys me that I never noted the registration of the AEC that I passed my test in.

Within weeks of passing my test a vacancy at Buckie arose, so the factory job was jacked in and my career on the buses began. Two weeks of route training and then I was let loose on my own. The fact that my father was my boss didn't really bother me, but it did bother others. During my first week I was taken aside by one of the senior drivers and told that when entering the drivers' mess room I would at times be conscious of conversations suddenly stopping, and any comments made within the drivers' room about management had not to be repeated to my father. I always respected that, but as mess rooms tended to be smoky places, with card schools and darts, and with a radio blaring music that suited the tastes of the more senior drivers rather than the rock stuff that I listened to, I didn't spend too much time in our bothy. I knew most of the drivers quite well anyway, even before I started work at the depot, as I had spent quite a bit of time travelling on buses to and from Portsoy when I was courting my wife to be. The last bus home was always a Buckie driver.

The depot allocation at that time included Albion Vikings NNV53, 54 and 79; Fords NT19, 24, 37, 57, 82, and 100; plus frontline coach (with radio!) Bedford Viceroy NW277. The Vikings would eventually go, as would the Viceroy and some of the early Fords, replaced by NT76, NT77, NT110, NT131, NT149, NT178, NPE74 and NPE102. There was still plenty of AECs left within the fleet, and these would regularly appear on changeovers, as would the occasional Leopard. Macduff had two ex Eastern Scottish AEC Reliances, and I always looked forward to getting them on changeovers. These 590 engined beasts were awesome, and none of the other AECs emitted the sounds that these two could produce. I also liked the early three-pedal Leopards with their low driving position and large flat steering wheel. I would be driving manual gearbox buses for around 3 years before experiencing a semi automatic for the first time, and even then they were few and far between.

The shift pattern in operation was good, with a mix of early, late and spreadover shifts. Early shifts would start at around 0530 and finish around 1330. Late shifts would start at 1500, finishing at 2330 unless there was a wedding hire or some other late-night festivity that necessitated overtime. Early and late shifts gave you decent day time to spend with the family or tend to the garden or other DIY chores. Spreadovers were less convenient, starting 0700 until around 0930, back from 1200 to 1400 on school or workers' runs, then the final stint from 1515 to around 1930. Your whole day was tied up, with very little spare time. Depots always had a 'sleeper in' shift – the first driver to be booked on. His first task was to mask (brew) the teapot in the bothy, then fill every bus radiator with water and start all the buses. On a cold morning the garage was just a mass of white smoke. If they didn't start, you would remove engine covers and locate the prime button on the pump. If that failed, you reallocated buses using whatever the depot engineer had marked as spare. A broom handle was also an important tool for starter motor problems! Of course, if you did have a sleep in you took over the shift and left someone else to go to the bakers.

I always tried to maintain running times, and being considerably younger than most of the others at the depot, there was a perception that I was a fast driver. I never really considered myself to be a fast driver, I just didn't hang around. Keen to make the job a success, and I suppose trying to prove my badge was no longer wet, I studied my fare book and quite quickly had fare stages and fares embedded in my head. During my first week this old lady came on at Buckie Square and to my mind she asked for Fyvie. In a flash I had the setright set to £1.50 or whatever the fare was, the ticket was issued and I asked the lady for her money. She handed over 5 pence. I said no, the fare was £1.50 to Fyvie. She responded, 'Ah'm no going to Fyvie eh, ah'm going to Ianstown eh. The fare is only 5 eh.' She never caught me out again – eh! One girl always came on and paid her 20p fare with a fiver. You would ask if she had the correct fare but no was always the answer – until the day she got £4.80 in 5p pieces. She always had the correct fare after that. I suspect many a driver has had to encounter that scenario. Local place names could also be problematic – one passenger asked for a single to Achinichee (Ach-ine-ichee) – could I find such a place in the fare book. I asked the passenger to point out the fare stage on my book – the proper name was Auchindachy. Then there was the lady who had forgotten her 'confession' pass – you had to laugh.

The work allocation took us west as far as Elgin, east to Aberdeen via Macduff, and south as far as Keith, with local duplicates (or poachers as my granny called them) and short workings. Parcel and newspaper traffic was quite considerable on our services, and we even carried coffins (empty of course) from the Aberdeen-based supplier to local undertakers. Locally we had a decent hire book, with pensioner groups, local welfare league football teams, and Highland dance groups using our services for evening and weekend hires, plus odd longer distance hires, Blackpool Illuminations, Edinburgh Airport, Largs, Ingliston market to name but a few that I did. We also got bucket and spade work from Aberdeen depot and other SBG companies. It wasn't uncommon to do an early shift on a Friday, home for a quick tea and change into your best uniform (you always kept a new one for hires, etc.), and into Aberdeen bus station with a 2200 departure for Blackpool. There were always one or two additional drivers allocated for sharing the driving, but it wasn't uncommon to do the trip alone because of mechanical problems with our Fords! Arriving in Blackpool in the early hours of Saturday, you would try and grab a few hours sleep before heading back from Blackpool at 1900, sometimes with a load, sometimes empty. Catching up on your sleep meant Sunday was a lost day. I have seen us drive empty from Buckie to Glasgow (staying at Mrs McGillivray's guest house at Stepps), take a load from Glasgow to Blackpool, and return empty all the way to Buckie. How they ever made money on these is a mystery. I even managed a stint on the day service to London during one of the rail strikes. From memory, we had NPE108 on the outward trip (it had one of those extremely high steering wheels) and with power steering failure from Birmingham it was a bit of a beast towards the end of the journey. It was flat out all the way there. Engineers at Stockwell were unable to repair the problem before the following morning so NPE75, having just completed the overnight service from Aberdeen, was checked for water and oil, mopped out and allocated to us for the return trip. Both these Leopards had fixed seats and no toilet – it must have been an uncomfortable trip for anyone accustomed to rail travel.

Returning to deckers – as I mentioned, neighbouring Elgin depot had two Lowlanders but they went not long after I passed my test. That was thought to be the end of deckers in the area, but quite surprisingly Elgin was allocated three of the five FLFs acquired by Northern. I decided that more for my own benefit I wanted to get my decker licence and after a few evenings behind the wheel of NRD5, I sat and passed my decker test. My licence now allowed me to drive any type bus rather than the previous single-deck restriction. Things would take a further dramatic change when, as a result of the SCOTMAP exercise, it was decided to transfer Aberdeen's allocation of one-year-old Olympians to the depots. Buckie was allocated TSO21X (NLO21) and although mainly for school contract work, the Olympian saw weekend service work to Aberdeen and occasional turns on the Buckie to Keith service. I was therefore quite glad that I had taken the decker test.

Did I enjoy my driving days? Without question, yes. Every day was different, every bus was different, you saw wildlife in the early morning, and you saw a different type of wildlife if you were on late shift. I wore my uniform and licence badges with immense pride, and I even participated in the driver of the year competition at Livingston MOTEC. After 8 years driving, I was promoted to Inspector – that was the career path in those days – but I hated every day of being an Inspector. I suppose, like most others, I would have wanted to be a DTS with my own depot but what with deregulation and privatisation, the management structure was completely overhauled and opportunities were at that time few and far between.

Were I 21 today would I be so keen to be a bus driver? I don't know is the honest answer. Driving should be just as enjoyable today as it was in 1975 – vehicles are far more advanced, with more thought given to driver comfort. Apparently the majority of shifts are long, though, with less early and late shifts. Health and safety – well, I won't even go there. Many bus drivers, especially in city and high population urban areas, might read this and see no comparison with the job they did or do today, but that was life working in a small depot.

Robert Carlyle learned to drive a bus and successfully passed the test for his role as a bus driver in the film Carla's Song. I remember listening to a radio interview where he was talking about his movie career, and he said that passing his PSV test was one of the best moments of his career, stating that only those who had passed the test would understand what he meant. I certainly understood what he was saying.

Where It All Started

My earliest recollection of our local buses was the blue and cream vehicles operated by Alexander's. Typical of the early ones I travelled on was this 1946 Burlingham bodied AEC Regal, fleet number A18. This Elgin-based vehicle is seen on the A96 just outside the Elgin depot. (*John Sinclair*)

New in 1937, this Alexander bodied Leyland TS7 lasted until 1963 but, as can be seen in this photo, this batch never received the yellow livery introduced during 1961. This view shows a line up of withdrawn vehicles at Aberdeen depot. A number of these ended their days in use as fairground transport.

These Burlingham bodied AEC Regals were the first vehicles I saw painted into the new yellow livery. Here NA16 and NA13 are at their home depot in Buckie during 1964, devoid of depot allocation plates and awaiting disposal. (*John Sinclair*)

Two early recipients of the yellow livery stand together at Elgin Bus Station. The one on the left is a 1946 Alexander bodied AEC Regal, NA26, while the one on the right is a 1950 Alexander bodied Leyland Tiger PS1, NPA184. (*John Sinclair*)

Seen at Dundee Bus Station is Forfar allocated NPA42, a 1947 Alexander bodied Leyland Tiger PS1. These Leyland buses typically had a life span of around twenty-four years, and even after that many saw further service as contractor buses.

Leyland supplied the Alexander company with the bulk of their single deck requirements for many years. The Leyland Tiger PS1 formed the backbone of the Northern-based allocation when the company was split in 1961. This 1948 example, NPA70, allocated to Rosehearty depot, is seen at Fraserburgh Bus Station.

Seen in Cullen Square, possibly when my father had gone home during layover time, is NPA91. I used to get a hurl in the cab of these when father was returning light to the garage at Buckie.

This was an unusual Leyland Tiger PS1 and certainly stood out during its time at Buckie depot as it had a full front cab rather than the half cab style of its contemporaries. NPA92 was acquired by Northern from Strachan's of Ballater when the company was taken over in 1965. (*John Sinclair*)

Another odd ball that was allocated to Buckie for a while was this former Sutherland's of Peterhead 1948 Duple bodied Leyland Tiger PS1, NPA200. I recall travelling to school on this bus – it was not liked by the clippies due to its heavy sliding door.

The NPB class Leyland OPS2/1 was originally designed as a front line coach when new in 1951. They were subsequently rebuilt to PS1 standard in 1961. This particular bus, NPB10, lasted until 1972. It is seen entering Aberdeen Bus Station late in its life.

Now these were something special. With their middle entrance door, passengers could sit up front alongside the driver. On the odd occasion one would operate the school bus run from Cullen to Buckie, there would be an unholy scramble to be first on board to bags the front seat. This view shows Elgin-based Alexander bodied Leyland Royal Tiger coaches NPC4 and NPC5 parked up at the Pinefield (Elgin) garage.

As well as the Alexander bodied Royal Tiger coaches, there was a small number of Leyland bodied ones in the Northern fleet. NPC30 is an example of the Leyland bodied model, new in 1952. (*John Sinclair*)

Here we have two Leyland Tiger Cub coaches, NPD7 and NPD10, both from the same batch, although one carries the traditional Northern coach livery of predominantly cream, while the other has been repainted in to the mostly yellow dual-purpose livery. Although allocated to Aberdeen depot, both are seen at the Elgin garage, presumably having completed express or limited stop services. I recall that these had sumptuous interiors, and I always remember the little red button on the gear stick which indicated they had twin speed rear axles. (*John Sinclair*)

The NPD class coaches were predominately allocated to Aberdeen. Special hires were operated to take fisherman home to Buckie and its neighbouring villages from Aberdeen on a Friday afternoon, returning to Aberdeen mid-morning on Monday. The Aberdeen allocated coach would sometimes be used for a school run on the Monday morning to cover for a 'docker', a vehicle in for routine maintenance. Here, NPD12 displays a local 'Buckie' window bill, suggesting it had been used for local service work. (*John Sinclair*)

I didn't travel on these Albion Aberdonian buses very often, but I do recall that they had cold leather style seats. Most drivers described them as underpowered, with a gear change akin to stirring porridge. Here, NNL22 rests at the Aberdeen garage on Gairn Terrace.

Double deckers were a rare sight in and around Buckie. However, Elgin depot did have an allocation of deckers over the years, and these would occasionally find themselves going as far as Buckie on duplicate journeys. Although carrying a Peterhead depot plate, ex Sutherland's NRC24 is seen at Elgin depot.

This 1955 AEC Reliance, fleet number NAC7, is typical of what my father drove on the route from Inverness to Aberdeen via the Coast. This view sees it awaiting its return journey at Aberdeen Bus Station, looking freshly painted. The route number, however, was not one associated with a journey to Buckie.

Elgin's NAC104 awaits its next turn of duty on stance two at the old Cumming Street bus station. (*John Sinclair*)

During the mid-1960s, Northern acquired a number of long established North East bus companies, and as a result a considerable number of non standard vehicles came into the fleet. Many were disposed of without actually being used, but some saw further use and even received fleet livery. This view at Aberdeen depot shows an ex Simpson's of Rosehearty Ford 570E with Duple Northern body. It was allocated fleet number NT5 when acquired in 1966 and survived with Northern until 1975.

NT6 was another former Simpson's coach, new to Simpson's during November 1964. This Plaxton bodied Ford 570E, seen arriving at Aberdeen bus station from the Buchan area, survived with Northern until 1976, when it was sold for scrap. (*John Sinclair*)

This former Simpson's Plaxton bodied Ford 676E was only a year old when acquired by Northern. Carrying fleet number NT7, it is seen late on in its life at Macduff depot, relegated to school duties. Like most of its contemporaries it was sold for scrap when withdrawn.

Another oddball, this time a former Burnett's of Mintlaw 1956 Plaxton bodied AEC Reliance. When it was acquired in 1967 it was allocated fleet number NAC5, and eked out a further nine years of service before being retired.

NAC15 was a one off with Northern. Although the company was allocated numerous Alexander bodied AEC Reliances when the main company split in 1961, only one Park Royal Reliance was allocated to Northern, the remaining nineteen going to the newly formed Midland company. NAC15 lasted in service until 1974, thereafter being used as a store/changing room by Ardallie Football Club near Ellon.

When I was a youngster staying in Cullen, the Huntly bus always fascinated me as it was a smaller bus than the ones driven by my father. I can just recall seeing a Bedford OB used on the service, but from 1964 this Duple Midland bodied Bedford VAS 1 was the regular performer. Here, NW265 awaits its departure before heading for Keith. (*John Sinclair*)

This view captures my school-day memories of Buckie depot, when we had to walk from the High School to the garage to get taken back home to Cullen. This mid-1960s view shows NA25, a 1946 AEC Regal in company with NAC257, a 1964 AEC Reliance.

The Era of My Employment

It was a vehicle identical to this, perhaps even this one, which I passed my PSV test in. These early AEC Reliance vehicles were extremely easy to drive. This view shows NAC96 in the parking area at Elgin's Pinefield depot.

There were still many AEC Reliances in the fleet when I started in 1975. This 1960 example, NAC186, was typical of the dual purpose style used on longer distance and local service work. This Aberdeen-allocated bus is seen at Elgin being readied for the trip to Inverness before returning to its home depot.

By the time I started with the company, these once front line coaches were relegated to school contract work as the manual door did not lend itself to one man operation. New in 1962, NAC206 saw service with Dundee depot before heading north to Elgin. Withdrawn in 1977, it was sold to the Turriff-based scrap merchant Len Kelbie, who in turn sold it to Lawson of Kirriemuir for transporting farm workers to and from the various fruit and potato sites in the Angus area.

Although all three vehicles carry the Alexander Y type body, they were completely different vehicles to drive. On the left is NPE8, a heavyweight Leyland Leopard; the centre vehicle is AEC Reliance NAC230; while the vehicle on the right is the lightweight rear engine Albion Viking NNV94. All three are seen at Aberdeen bus station.

NAC257 was originally allocated to Buckie depot when new in 1964. It had been reallocated to Peterhead depot before I started, but returned during my time as a driver as an emergency allocation to cover for broken down Fords. There were two batches of these AEC Reliance coaches, and although they appeared identical, you soon discovered they had significant differences. One batch had vacuum brakes, needing a bit of effort to bring them to a halt. The second batch had air brakes and only needed the lightest touch of the brake pedal to stop them. If you were unfamiliar with the latter type, you soon discovered how ferocious the brakes were the first time you stopped and threw any standing passengers forward. They were lovely motors to drive, even though the heating system was substandard for the North East winter climate.

These were my all time favourites to drive – six big engine AEC Reliances that came to Northern from the Edinburgh-based Eastern Scottish fleet. One of the six had a short life, being burnt out at Lhanbryde. Two were eventually allocated to Macduff depot and these would be used frequently on the route from Aberdeen to Elgin via the Coast. This view shows NAC262 near Dallas on a farewell AEC Tour organised by the Aberdeen Transport Society. I always looked forward to getting one of the pair on a changeover. It was hoped that one would be saved for preservation but more about that later.

The rear engine lightweight Albion Viking was seen as a suitable low cost vehicle for rural routes. They had crash gearboxes and rookie drivers dreaded being allocated a Viking. Once you had mastered the gearbox, they were a very simple and easy vehicle to drive. Luggage space was restricted to small side locker so parcels would be carried inside the saloon. NNV33 is seen heading out of Buckie on the journey to Elgin.

This 1970 view of Aberdeen depot shows the rear grille arrangement of the Viking, demonstrated by NNV43. In the background is one of the former Sutherland Peterhead Duple coaches, and a recently acquired ex Western SMT 1956 Leyland PD2 double decker, HSD13.

The Vikings were ideal for short local routes and were a common sight along the north-east coast. NNV45, allocated to Macduff, is seen at Buckie depot, awaiting time for its return home. The car parking area at the east of the garage was reserved for the District Traffic Superintendent and the Depot Engineer.

Another Macduff Viking at Buckie, this time NNV46, picks up passengers on the service to Aberdeen. The journey to Aberdeen would take three hours from Buckie, work that was really unsuited to the Viking. This view has also captured a taxi from that era, one of a number of Fiat saloons operated by Buckie-based Moravian Taxis.

During my time at Buckie the depot had an allocation of three Vikings, NNV53, NNV54 and NNV79. Here, NNV53 is seen at the depot when relatively new as the chrome bumper was apparently too heavy for the Y Type fibreglass front and all were removed at an early stage. (*John Sinclair*)

Sister NNV54 is seen here on a short working from the local AEI (later Thorn Lighting) bulb factory to Portgordon, taking workers home after their day shift. Buckie-based driver Bill Pattinson is behind the wheel.

Late afternoon would usually see some vehicles being refuelled before working on until near midnight. This view shows Macduff-allocated NNV70 on the pumps at Buckie depot. It would then operate a local school run before heading back out on service, ending up at its home depot after a number of driver changeovers.

NNV79 was the newest of the three Buckie Vikings. Although pretty much identical, all three had different driving characteristics. This one was the slowest of the three, pretty much a proverbial plug of a bus. At least two former Northern Vikings are now in preservation.

Elgin-allocated NNV85, seen at Elgin depot, was one of the last new Vikings to enter service with Northern. The Vikings had on average a thirteen-year life before being withdrawn. Most were sold for scrap.

During 1972 Northern acquired six additional Vikings from Eastern Scottish. Acquired when seven years old, they were unusual in having only thirty-four seats compared with the standard forty on all other Vikings. They were quickly re-seated to increase capacity and entered service in a mainly cream livery, as shown on NNV94; the original green flash of Eastern Scottish was simply painted yellow.

Coaches never really formed a large part of the Northern operation, hires being operated by dual-purpose semi coaches. A small number of traditional coaches were operated, and in due course most depots would have an allocation of at least one coach for private hires. When I started at Buckie the depot coach was NW277, a 1970 Bedford VAM70 with Duple Viceroy body, and sister vehicle to NW274 shown here. These were noisy coaches, with heavy steering and soft brakes, not the most refined vehicles I have ever driven. At least the Buckie one had a radio, which was quite a luxury back in 1975.

NW277 is seen in later years, parked up for the day at Baxter's. With a manual door, it was only suitable for school duties and would have operated from the Garmouth/Kingston area to Milnes High School in Fochabers. Elgin depot would leave their school buses at Baxter's, thereby reducing the operational cost of running the contracts. (*John Sinclair*)

The backbone of the Buckie allocation during the 1970s were Alexander bodied Fords. My very first duty involved doing a local school run with either NT19 or NT24 from Findochty to Buckie High school. Although these buses had a seating capacity of fifty-three, it was not uncommon to carry up to eighty pupils on one journey. In this view, NT19 is seen heading for Keith on a cold snowy morning.

With Aberdeen-based Ian Thompson at the wheel, NT22 heads back into the platforms at Aberdeen bus station for its next turn of duty. The chrome Ford badges on these vehicles didn't stay on for long! (*John Sinclair*)

The three big Fords allocated to Buckie during the mid-1970s were NT19, NT24 and NT37. In this view at the depot, they carry the original coach livery.

As part of the seven-year body overhaul and repaint programme, all bus-seated vehicles were repainted into the mainly yellow livery. This was supposedly a marketing ploy so that customers knew they were travelling on a coach or dual purpose vehicle rather than a basic service bus. The idea was good, but would only work if bus-seated vehicles were restricted to short distance journeys. Unfortunately, bus-seated vehicles still found their way onto longer distance routes. NT24 and NT19 are seen carrying their all-yellow livery.

This view shows how well the Northern depots looked after their vehicles. The photo was taken minutes before NT24 was delivered to the central workshops for its seven-year overhaul. The photo demonstrates a clean, straight vehicle despite years of hard work.

Some batches of Fords were noisier than others, and I recall that the VRG-L batch fell into that category. This one, NT36, allocated to Elgin, had dual purpose seats more suited to the four-hour trip from Inverness to Aberdeen. (*John Sinclair*)

Fraserburgh-based NT39 was the only Y Type to carry this revised style livery. It is seen at Fraserburgh depot on a cold winter morning.

From 1973 onwards the Fords had an improved interior design, with a warmer orange-coloured moquette used for the seats. The short wheelbase R1014 models delivered from 1973 to 1975 had no power steering and were quite heavy. Macduff-allocated NT56 is seen at Buckie depot during layover.

Most depots got at least one new Ford every year and Buckie was no exception. For its 1973 allocation, it received this forty-one-seat Ford R1014, NT57. It was used regularly on private hires so where possible it would be kept away from school runs, vandalism being common on school buses. Here it is seen on the route between Dufftown and Keith, operating a Saturday only service from Aberlour driven by Buckie driver Bert Masson.

Bay four at the old Elgin Cumming Street bus station was the spare bay, where up to twelve vehicles could be found during the off peak. In this view we see Ford R1014 NT60 (minus its Ford badge) and Albion Vikings NNV85, NNV90 and NNV27.

Seen soon after delivery in 1973 is Aberdeen allocated NT66, a Ford R1014 with an Alexander forty-five seat body.

Another 1973 delivery was NT70, a fifty-three-seat Ford R1114. It is seen at Inverness Bus Station about to depart for Elgin. For whatever reason, the fleet number is not in the usual plate style, simply transfers applied on the lower panel. (*John Sinclair*)

Deliveries for 1974 included four forty-five-seat Ford Duple coaches, ordered specifically for tour work. Unlike all previous and subsequent deliveries of Fords, this batch did not carry consecutive number plates that matched the fleet number. Parked up at Gairn Terrace depot immediately after delivery from the Blackpool coachworks are NT75, RRG347N, and NT77, RRG348N.

The other two Duples from the 1974 batch were NT76, PRS718M, and NT78, PRS720M. None of the four had power steering when new, but this was retrofitted after their first year of tour work. Here we see NT76 on delivery day at Aberdeen.

After only one year of tour work, these coaches were transferred to depots where there was significant private hire work. NT76 initially went to Fraserburgh but was subsequently transferred to Buckie, where it met up with sister NT77. Both were used on hires and tours as well as normal service work.

Within each batch of buses there was usually at least one that stood out either in a positive way or in a negative way. NT96 was one of those that was disliked by everyone who had the misfortune to drive it as it was dour, heavy to steer, and extremely noisy. It is seen on this occasion passing through Fordyce. Parcels generated quite a bit of income and a number of packages can be seen on the front seat. Although the Y Type had a decent sized boot, parcels would regularly be carried in the saloon as water ingress in the boot was not uncommon – and it also saved the driver a bit of time when delivering to the parcel agents along the route.

1975 saw a variety of new Fords arriving. Among the first were half a dozen fifty-three-seat buses including NT99 and NT100, seen here at Aberdeen before delivery to their new home depots. Although bus-seated, Buckie-allocated NT100 was a regular performer on the Elgin to Aberdeen route. It was an extremely reliable bus and, for a Ford, a very good performer on what was a long distance route.

The next batch for 1975 included a number of dual purpose seated Fords. They had particularly high head restraints which impeded forward vision for passengers. NT110 is seen operating the Buckie town service. Noteworthy are the houses in the background – these were aluminium clad 'multicom' houses built in 1968 by Weir's of Coatbridge at a cost of £2,800 each.

As well as the daily service from Cullen and Buckie to Keith, the depot operated a Saturday only service from Aberlour to Keith. This was a particularly scenic route, especially during winter. Awaiting a summer early morning departure from Aberlour is NT131, a short forty-one-seat Ford R1014.

Another view of NT131, this time on the wash bed at Buckie depot. Every bus was hand washed every night by the night shunter, while the interiors would be swept out and washed by the night cleaner. The shunter would also fuel every bus before finalising the parking arrangements to suit the following day's allocation.

Winter was always a worry for drivers, but no services were ever cancelled based on weather forecasts. You simply turned up for work, set off on your duty, and hoped you would not get stuck. Here, NT131 has just returned to its home depot after completing its run to Keith. On that particular route, Albion Vikings were the preferred bus when there had been significant snowfall, due to their narrower wheelbase and greater weight above the rear wheels.

1976 saw further deliveries of coaches from Duple, the majority with forty-nine seats but including four with a capacity of only forty-five. One of the latter is NT135, seen when new in an unusual variant of the standard livery with cream windscreen surround.

Seen in later life carrying standard livery, Montrose-allocated NT135 passes under the Fettercairn Arch on a local service journey.

One of the forty-nine-seat coaches from the 1976 delivery, Elgin-allocated NT143, heads into Portknockie from the east. At this time, traffic had to cross two tight railway bridges in the village, but like the trains before them the bridges have now gone.

The last batch from the 1976 Duple order had revised front ends like NT147, seen here climbing out of Findochty on its journey to Aberdeen. The Moray Firth in the background looks particularly cold despite the sunshine as Dennis Kirkby heads towards Aberdeen.

Buckie's front line coach from 1976 was NT149, a forty-nine-seat Duple bodied Ford R1114. On service 96, it is seen dropping down from Aultmore towards Ryeriggs on the Braes of Enzie between Keith and Buckie. In this view it carries its original livery, displaying the Bluebird logo on the side.

In the lead up to bus deregulation in 1986, the Scottish Bus Group undertook various research projects to streamline services to ensure routes were sustainable. One of the new routes introduced was the 396 between Keith and Banff. Here we see NT149 operating the service on the outskirts of Portsoy, carrying only the driver and an Inspector, perhaps demonstrating all that was wrong with how the research was managed locally.

With the Inverness-bound train on the platform, NT149 awaits its passengers before departing for Buckie. The service is now operated under Council contract by Deveron Coaches, but at the time of writing the service is under threat of cancellation due to budget cuts.

Contract services were operated for a number of employers in the area, including the bulb factory, the scampi factory and the boat builders, all based at Buckie, as well as the Baxter's food factory at Fochabers. Cullen Square was the changeover point for Baxter's employees who stayed beyond Cullen to the east. Buckie's NT149 has operated the journey from Fochabers as far as Cullen, with Macduff's NT138 completing the homeward journey for the factory girls.

A final view of NT149, late on in its life, operating the 308 Buckie to Aberdeen via Foggie express. By this time, the coach is carrying its third livery style. It is seen between Cornhill and Aberchirder (Foggie to the locals!) Following withdrawal, NT149 was used by the company as an exhibition bus before being sold for scrap.

As well as Duple coaches, the company purchased a batch of unusual bus-seated Duples. Although the basic body style was similar to the coach variant, the interior was extremely basic and spartan. These were delivered in 1977 and NT154 clearly demonstrates the basic seating fitted to this batch. These were known as Duple E Types, a name with clearly no connection to a famous car.

Seen arriving at Aberdeen bus station when relatively new is Stonehaven-allocated NT157. (*John Sinclair*)

This later view of NT157 shows it carrying the revised company name and also promoting the Scottish Bus Group slogan, 'Best Bus Around' – hardly appropriate for a shed on wheels! Behind the wheel is Alex Gamrie, who transferred to Alexander's when they acquired Simpson's of Rosehearty. Based at Gardenstown, Alex Ritchie worked mainly in the Buchan area but for a short period he was allocated a duty that saw him operate to Elgin.

Travelling along the main A96, which passes through the centre of Elgin, NT172 heads for Lhanbryde, Garmouth and Kingston. The stricken Dennison truck in the photo was an unusual type truck for this area.

The last new Ford to be allocated to Buckie depot was NT178, delivered in 1977. This was a fairly hard-worked bus, running most days from around 0600 to 2200, including a peak return journey from Aberdeen – quite a thrash with a full load.

Having operated from Macduff to the Fochabers-based Baxter's food factory, NT185 rests outside Buckie depot. The driver was no doubt having a quick cup of tea and a rowie (buttery) before heading to Portsoy to uplift his contingent of school kids for Banff Academy. As the office light is on, it is assumed that the 'mannie' (the boss) was at work when the photo was taken.

Despite their unreliability, Northern acquired a further five Duple bodied Ford coaches in 1979 from Alexander's Fife. These were less than five years old when acquired and were allocated across the various depots. NT196 was allocated to Elgin and in this view it is seen leaving Fochabers, bound for Aberdeen via Buckie and Macduff.

Another ex Fifer to come north was NT199, allocated to Macduff and seen turning into Findochty soon after acquisition but before a destination screen had been fitted. It was common practice throughout the Scottish Bus Group to display paper destination bills on the windscreen when no appropriate screen was available.

The last new Fords to be purchased were five Ford service saloons with Alexander forty-five-seat bodies. Like the previous batch, these had a front-mounted inclined engine, whereas all other Fords had the upright front mounted engine. The latter type could be recognised with the revised front grille arrangement as demonstrated on Elgin's NT203.

The company looked at various vehicle types to replace the Fords and this Dennis Lancet was one of two experimental buses purchased in 1984. ND1 had a Perkins engine with fully automatic Allison gearbox and was a bit agricultural-like, even compared with the Fords. During its time with Northern, it was allocated to quite a few depots. At the time of this photo it was Elgin-based and is seen at Elgin depot, being driven by Ronnie Dean.

The second of the trial experimental buses purchased in 1984 was NA1, a Volvo B57 with Alexander Y Type body. Because of its awkward front engine layout the driver sat well back from the windscreen, a strange feeling for someone accustomed to the layout of the Ford or Leopard. One thing was for sure – it couldn't half shift, as some car drivers found out at the traffic lights in Aberdeen when I drove it on the 308 service. This was the last Alexander Y type body built.

Two batches of Leyland Tiger buses with Alexander P Type bodies would arrive during 1983 and 1984. The second batch had Gardner engines rather than the Leyland unit fitted to the earlier ones. Stonehaven-allocated NBT24 from the second batch is seen heading south through Inverbervie on the service to Dundee.

NBT26 carries a predominately yellow front livery compared with the black windscreen surround carried by NBT 24 in the previous image. Depot codes had given way to area codes by the late 1980s and Huntly-based NBT26 displays M for Moray after the fleet number. It is seen in Keith Square operating a short working from Elgin to Huntly, its last working of the day.

Northern started long distance cross-Border express journeys in the mid-1970s and over the years acquired small batches of coaches suitable for that purpose. These vehicles didn't just do express services though, as demonstrated in this view. Metroliner NCM6 is seen acting as a school bus replacement after the Olympian behind had failed on its journey from Stonehaven to Portlethen.

It was common practice throughout the Scottish Bus Group to hold open days where members of the public could view new deliveries as well as vintage buses. One such open day was held at Elgin and available for public inspection was this Metroliner coach, NCM10.

NCT9, originally ASA9Y, passes through Ellon on its journey from Peterhead to Aberdeen. These Duple bodied Leyland Tigers were well appointed internally and used on long distance express service work before being demoted to local service duties. This batch was renowned for their turn of speed.

A rare sight at that time was a Citylink liveried vehicle on regular service work. Heading out of Portknockie is NCT11, operating service 305 to Aberdeen with Buckie driver James Runcie. It would either have been a substitute vehicle following a breakdown or returning to its home depot in Aberdeen after perhaps being borrowed by Buckie or Elgin depot for a long distance hire. (*James Mair*)

NCT33 was an ex Midland Leyland Tiger with Alexander TE coach-style body. Originally carrying the traditional Midland livery, it is seen here wearing the corporate Scottish Citylink livery and fitted with revised seating introduced specifically for Citylink coaches. It is seen here at Glack Crossroads on its return to Aberdeen depot after being borrowed for a hire.

As well as the unique Volvo B57 mentioned earlier, Northern trialled a Dennis Lancet with Alexander Y Type body. This trial resulted in an order for five further Lancets, but these would carry the Alexander P Type body, as seen with Moray-allocated ND6. After further service with a Derbyshire operator, ND6 was acquired by a Stoke-based preservationist and has been restored in full Northern livery.

When I started with Northern in 1975, the only local-based deckers were two Albion Lowlanders based at Elgin. NRE1 is seen at Elgin Bus Station. Inspector Sammy Fraser and the clippie discuss its next run, probably a short duplicate to Fochabers going by the screen.

Five former Alexander Midland Bristol FLF deckers came to Northern in 1979 in a surprise transfer. These had been new to Eastern National in 1966 and had been extremely well used before coming north. Three of these worked for a time at Elgin, and NRD3 is seen carrying promotional material for a local distillery. As far as everyone was concerned these would be the last deckers to come north so having only a single deck licence, I decided to get my decker licence while I had the chance and passed my test on NRD5. Little did we know that more deckers would follow a few years later.

To supplement the decker allocation, five former Central SMT Daimler Fleetlines were acquired in 1976. Initially used on Aberdeen city services on the Culter to Dyce corridor (known by local drivers as the track), they were eventually cascaded to other depots such as Montrose, where NRF4 is seen.

Northern's first new deckers since 1963 arrived during 1978 in the form of eight ECW bodied Fleetlines. These carried Leyland badges rather than the Daimler badges carried on previously acquired Fleetlines. These were bought specifically for Aberdeen city services, but during times of vehicle shortages they could be found out in the sticks. NRF23 is seen about to head back to Aberdeen from Buckie on the 60-mile 308 express service – and they wondered why passengers stopped using the service.

More new deckers started appearing from 1981, based on Leyland Olympian running gear, some with Alexander bodies, others with ECW bodies. NLO6 is an Alexander bodied example and carries all-over advertising for McEwans Export.

I always considered the ECW body more attractive than the square Alexander product. These were again allocated to Aberdeen when new, but after only one year they were farmed out to other depots as a cost saving measure on school runs. This ECW bodied example, NLO13, is seen at Tipperty near Ellon on its journey from Fraserburgh to Aberdeen.

Even after a year on Aberdeen city service work, these ECW deckers were still in excellent condition and certainly turned heads in areas where no deckers had previously operated. Elgin initially received four and they could generally be found on the Lossiemouth and Burghead routes. NLO14 awaits a driver at Pinefield depot in Elgin before going back into service.

Two of the four Olympians at Elgin immediately after transfer. Both NLO15 and NLO16 have slip board destinations as local screens had still to be fitted.

As part of the Scotmap process Buckie was allocated a decker for school duties and service work, supposedly to reduce the need for duplication at peak times. Surprisingly, we received NLO21, transferred from Aberdeen. Its allocation to Buckie even warranted the local newspaper to send a reporter and photographer to mark the occasion. By the time it came to Buckie the upper deck front hopper windows had been replaced with single glass windows – apparently they were prone to falling out, not something you wanted when carrying school pupils. With the Setright ticket machine on the rack and my conductor's bag on the dash, NLO21 is ready for its next service. Although primarily used for schools, it did see service work and was required on a Sunday night for a return journey to Aberdeen due to capacity issues.

Macduff received two of the ECW bodied Olympians, NLO14 and NLO24, and they would often meander up the coast on service work. NLO24 is seen at the top of Strathlene Brae, between Findochty and Portessie.

From the end of January 1983 co-ordinated services in Aberdeen were operated jointly by Northern and Grampian Transport. For these services a livery based on Grampian Transport's livery with Grampian Scottish fleetnames was applied to vehicles from both companies. For these services, Northern operated standard Alexander bodied Olympians and some Leyland Nationals. While these may have ventured to the suburbs, it was rare to see them beyond the City boundary, so it was quite an event when NLO33 was allocated to the 305 service from Aberdeen to Elgin to cover for a vehicle shortage at Aberdeen. Here it is seen passing under the disused railway viaduct at Cullen. This particular duty saw the bus and driver have a break in Buckie before heading back to Aberdeen. Even more unusual was the allocation of a conductor for the journey as the vehicle was fitted with autofare equipment. (*James Mair*)

A second shot of NLO33, with driver Duncan Smith at the wheel and the conductor on the platform. This photo was taken between Cullen and Portknockie. (*James Mair*)

Following deregulation in 1986, Northern introduced a City Bus livery for services that competed with Grampian Transport. NLO36, carrying the City Bus livery, is seen in Aberdeen working service 59 to Faulds Gate.

Following deregulation, Grampian Transport started competing services to various destinations beyond the city boundary. In what must have been an excellent coup for Grampian Transport, they managed to advertise their services on the big advertising boards within Aberdeen Bus Station. In an attempt to hide the advert, NLO37 has been strategically parked in the hope that Northern's passengers would not be tempted to take their custom to this new service provider.

In standard yellow livery, NLO38 operates a local town service in Ellon before heading back to Aberdeen.

New in 1983, NLO42 carries the final version of Northern's livery before the company would be acquired by Stagecoach. It is seen entering the temporary bus station at Elgin during the construction of the St Giles shopping centre.

All-over advertising was and still is a means of generating additional income. NLO54 is advertising the local Hawco car sales business, and is seen entering Elgin Bus Station for a journey to Speyside.

In readiness for deregulation, Northern splashed out on a large intake of new deckers, all Leyland Olympians, all with Alexander bodies, but some in City Bus livery for Aberdeen city services and some fitted with coach seats for longer distance service work. This was the line-up at Hazlehead for the official launch.

The line-up from the other side, showing the six coach-seated examples.

The coach seated examples could be found on medium distance routes such as Peterhead and Fraserburgh to Aberdeen. NLO63 is seen in Ellon, passing the now demolished Mercury Hotel.

Coach-seated Olympians such as NLO66 also ventured on longer distance services such as the Aberdeen to Inverness route. When seen in Huntly, the route was designated an express route, allocated route number 960, and operated under the Scottish Citylink banner. Noteworthy are the two Granada taxis operated by Shearers and both carrying 666 plates.

Further coach-seated examples would arrive the following year. NLO88 was the penultimate new decker to be delivered to Northern. It is seen here in Stonehaven.

Back to single deckers now. My first experience of Leopards was on a changeover at Macduff. Having driven Fords, Albions and AECs, the Leopard looked an intimidating beast with its large flat steering wheel, low driving position, and a gearbox that I had never experienced. Once on the open road I had nothing to fear, as they were fantastic buses to drive. One of the first batch, NPE4, is seen at Buckie heading for Elgin.

The second batch arrived in 1967 and was outwardly similar to the earlier batch. Internally, they had different coloured seats and trim. NPE6 is seen here departing Perth Bus Station on a hire or long distance duplicate.

Later in its life, NPE6 is seen near Swordanes, Inverboyndie, near Banff. The original steering wheel plastic has obviously broken at some point, with yellow insulating tape used to try and provide a smooth surface. That was fine until the wheel came back at speed; if the driver was not careful, the tape joins would shred his fingers.

Elgin had two of the fifty-three-seat Leopards from the 1971 delivery, NPE24 and NPE28. From memory, NPE24 was allocated to Macduff but as it wasn't clocking up the required mileage, it was soon despatched to Elgin. Boarding out of the designated stances, driver Jack Scorgie uplifts his passengers before setting off for Lossiemouth.

The last new Leopards to come to Northern were a batch of five fifty-three-seat Alexander bodied saloons delivered in 1982. NPE40, allocated to Macduff, is seen when new and devoid of fleetnames, outside Buckie depot. This batch received fleet numbers that had previously been allocated to a batch of ex Central SMT Leopards acquired in 1976 and withdrawn in 1980.

59

The first proper heavyweight coaches came to the fleet in 1977. These were Duple bodied Leyland Leopards, the first semi automatic gearbox Leopards in the fleet. Elgin's allocation included NPE44 and NPE45. The former carried an unusual version of the livery during the transition between Northern and Northern Scottish, as seen here at Elgin depot.

Another view of NPE44, this time at Buckpool, with Aberdeen-based driver George (Dod) Hay at the wheel.

Another from the 1977 delivery was NPE46, seen later in life at Invercauld Road, Braemar.

Towards the end of the Northern company, some vehicles carried the Bluebird Northern name, as demonstrated by NPE47 as it heads into Aberdeen city centre from Ellon. As part of the ongoing bodywork maintenance programme, a lot of the chrome body trim had been removed.

NPE49 departs Aberdeen bus station, bound for New Deer in rural Aberdeenshire.

With Elgin driver Sandy Badenoch at the wheel, NPE50 crosses the River Spey at Fochabers. Going by the ice on the river it must have been a very cold day.

NPE50 in warmer times, operating a hire from Dufftown Railway Station. In 1984 John Begg of Grampian Railtours started running the Northern Belle excursion train to Dufftown using Nightrider train stock that lay over in Aberdeen during the day. NPE50 was used to transport guests the short distance to Glenfiddich Distillery and up into Dufftown. Like many of its contemporaries, the chrome work on NPE50 had been removed and replaced with basic beading.

Passing through the coastal village of Portessie, NPE51 skirts the Moray Firth on what must be one of the most scenic coastal journeys that can be made by bus.

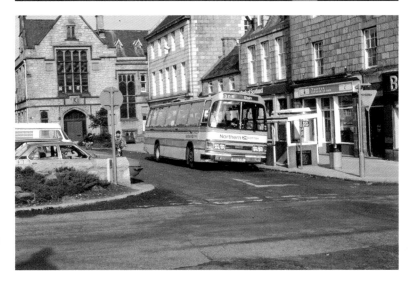

Elgin driver Grigor Winchester bides his time at Huntly Square with NPE53 on his return from Aberdeen.

NPE54 is seen at Aberdeen when new, resplendent in its original Northern livery with the Bluebird displayed on the side panel.

The Alexander T Type body was chosen for the next batch of Leopards, delivered during 1979. Departing Elgin depot on its first day of service is NPE60, being driven by Charlie Riddoch.

A trio of T Types, photographed from the upstairs offices at Northern's now closed Guild Street offices. NPE62, NPE64 and NPE63 await their next turn of duty.

The T Type Leopard
was a useful dual
purpose vehicle, suited
to the demands of
longer distance local
services, private hire
work, and longer
distance summer
services to the usual
coastal holiday
delights of Blackpool,
Scarborough and
the like. NPE62 is
seen nearer to home
however at Aberdeen
Bus Station.

This shot was
taken on 1 January
1980, when a
comprehensive
network of services
was operated even
on Christmas Day
and New Year's
Day. NPE63 has just
uplifted a passenger
outside the ex
Servicemen's Club in
Elgin before the long
trek to Aberdeen via
the Coast.

By the late 1980s
NPE68 had
transferred to Moray
from its original
Stonehaven allocation
and is seen turning
into the depot at
Macduff.

Other 1979 deliveries included a batch of Duple bodied Leopards, similar to the 1977 batch. Following a fairly extensive body rebuild, NPE70 is seen in Aberdeen with all chrome work apart from headlamp surrounds removed. This bus demonstrates another late variation of the Northern livery, emphasising its Bluebird Northern parentage.

For long distance express services to the likes of Corby, a new Express livery was introduced. They did, however, stray onto non-express routes, as shown in this wintry scene at Cullen when NPE72 was operating the 5A service from Elgin to Aberdeen via the Coast. The 'A' signified that the route diverted via Fordyce.

Another Leopard from the same batch was also treated to the Express livery. In this view it had been 'hijacked' from its Aberdeen home depot and was being used on the service from Buckie to Keith. It was always a bit exciting when you got an unusual vehicle such as NPE75 for your shift.

NPE96 is another hijacked Leopard, again operating on the Buckie to Keith service. This had been borrowed from Aberdeen for a long distance hire but managed to find itself working on the Braes of Enzie on a Sunday afternoon. Buckie driver George Pirie was the lucky driver on that day.

NPE97 loads at Fochabers Square on its way to Aberdeen via Huntly with Bob Grant behind the wheel.

This fine Duple bodied Leopard was borrowed by Buckie depot when new for a hire to Blackpool. You felt king of the road when heading out of town with this beast. NPE100 had a short life, being stolen from Aberdeen and written off following a collision with a building.

The only new Leopard allocated to Buckie was NPE102. Fitted with wheel trims and Leyland Leopard badges, this was the pride of the depot. School duties were avoided to minimise vandal damage. In this view the cleaners are aboard, preparing it for a private hire. This vehicle is now preserved – more details follow later in this book.

The last new Duple bodied Leopards for Northern included NPE109, seen crossing Buckie Square on route to Aberdeen.

Probably the most modern buses to be allocated in the Northern area were the Leyland Nationals delivered new in 1980. The first three of the batch, NPN1, NPN2 and NPN3, were allocated to Elgin for town service work. With their easy access and well-thought-out driver's cab, they were well liked by passengers and drivers. In this view NPN1 has strayed to Buckie on the scampi workers' contract from Elgin, returning home at 2200 after the evening shift finished. It would not be unfair to say that passengers travelling on the bus the following morning would have known that fish processors had travelled in it the night before!

Sister vehicle NPN2 is seen in Elgin with Bob Wildgoose operating one of the town service routes.

The final one from the Elgin trio, NPN3, is seen on the High Street in Elgin working a town service journey. Although that area of the High Street remains largely unchanged apart from it being one way, buses no longer operate on the High Street.

NPN6 was transferred to Macduff for operating the local town service, but it did at times venture up the coast as far as Buckie. Here, it heads back to Macduff with the boat yard buildings in the background.

Behind the Wheel

The next selection shows the author behind the wheel. This view taken at Portknockie shows Leopard NPE2 bound for Aberdeen. With a slight incline after the stop, it would have been a first gear start with a straight through change into second before progressing up the box. Getting the revs right for a quick change avoided any embarrassing crunching noises (*James Mair*)

In this view, I am operating the local Buckie town service with NT82, a forty-five-seat Ford R1014. This was one of the early batches without power steering but truth be told it was a decent bus to drive and was a reliable member of the fleet. (*James Mair*)

Me and my boys! This Eastern Scottish open top Bristol was borrowed for the Elgin depot open day during the summer of 1985. This shot was taken at Portessie prior to the decker returning to Edinburgh.

One of those days you don't forget – a new bus and you are the first to drive it in service! As mentioned in an earlier chapter, NPE102 was the only new Leyland Leopard to be allocated to Buckie depot and most probably was the only new Leyland ever to be allocated. It is seen at Macduff heading back towards Buckie and I recall that father was waiting at the depot to make sure I hadn't put a scratch on his new bus! I had a long association with NPE102, as will be evident towards the end of this book. (*James Mair*)

NA1 was one of two experimental buses bought by Northern and allocated to Aberdeen depot when new. It was therefore rare for non-city drivers to drive these vehicles, but I was fortunate on one occasion to get the Volvo for the journey from Aberdeen to Buckie on the express 308 route. It really was different from everything else I had driven and had a remarkable turn of speed, something I made full use of during my shift. (*James Mair*)

Trips away from the home patch were usually limited to summer duplicates for the main Aberdeen depot, but occasionally you landed something different, as I did on this occasion. This was a hire from Elgin and Nairn to the Burrell Collection in Glasgow and for the hire I had new Metroliner NCM11, seen entering the gates at Pollock Country Park. (*James Mair*)

What Happens to Old Buses?

Like all other motor vehicles, buses and coaches can have mechanical problems and sometimes this necessitates a tow back to the depot. Various forms of support vehicles have been operated over the years, some purpose built, others converted from buses no longer suitable for further passenger carrying service. Within the Northern area, only four depots originally had tow vehicles – Elgin, Peterhead, Aberdeen and Dundee. For many a year the Elgin tow truck was this Leyland Bull, fleet number L127. It is now preserved.

Peterhead depot had at one time this Leyland TS8 tow truck, cut down from a single deck bus in 1959, originally WG8107, P528, new in 1939. Now preserved, N205L has spent more of its life as a tow truck than as a bus. It is seen inside Peterhead depot. (*John Sinclair*)

When deemed no longer suitable for further services, buses are usually scrapped, either by the operating company as a source of spares for other vehicles or by professional dismantlers. Some buses and coaches have, however, had a second life, usually in a non-PSV role. This ex Northern AEC Reliance from the ARG.B batch was being used as a site hut at Fordoun by NACAP Ltd when photographed in 1981.

Another former Northern AEC Reliance, NAC246, was subsequently acquired by Forres Academy and used for local outings. This bus has been saved and awaits restoration at the Scottish Vintage Bus museum based at Lathalmond.

Earlier in the book, I mentioned the potential saving of one of the ex Eastern Scottish AEC Reliances that came to Northern – well, this is it. After being withdrawn from service it received the statutory all-grey repaint and was despatched to Arbroath depot, where most of the withdrawn stock was stored. Lines of withdrawn buses must have been a temptation to the local vandals as most suffered window breakages during their stay. NAC262 had always been a favourite, not just for me but also for a couple of colleagues who shared an interest in buses. We therefore decided to try and get NAC262 back on the road.

After many weekends travelling to Arbroath depot, we eventually managed to return NAC262 to reasonable condition. This involved replacing most of the glass, sourcing a replacement front panel and fitting a replacement starter and batteries. This photo shows what we achieved, but sadly we never pursued the purchase of the bus and, like most others that were on site, it was eventually broken up.

A general view of Arbroath depot taken in 1982, showing a number of Albion Vikings awaiting final disposal. NNV14 is in all grey livery, with sisters NNV3, NNV5 and NNV89 alongside.

Partly cannibalised to keep others going, the next journey for these Vikings would have been to the breaker's yard.

For a short while Elgin depot resembled a breaker's yard when some of the early Fords were withdrawn and partly stripped of mechanical components to keep others going. Tucked into the corner are the two Duple Viceroy bodied Ford coaches delivered in 1972, carrying fleet numbers NT28 and NT29.

The Fords proved to be extremely unreliable, suffering everything from minor failures to full blown engine failures. As a result, most depots retained one of their withdrawn Albion Vikings for towing duties. In this view, Buckie's NNV54 is towing Ford NT57 to Aberdeen for repair following a major engine failure compounded by an electrical fault that caused smoke damage below the windscreen. I always enjoyed driving the tow bus but never liked steering the vehicle being towed.

Not everything was time expired when sold, as can be seen in this view. When less than two years old, NPE81 and four similar vehicles were transferred to Highland Omnibuses. This view taken at Buckie shows the Leopard in full Highland livery but still in the ownership of Northern.

Visitors

BUS653K was the first Volvo B58 to enter service in Britain, initially used by Volvo as a demonstrator. During its stay with Northern it operated on a number of routes, including a trip to New Deer according to the paper window bills. Remarkably, this vehicle still survives, although the Alexander Y Type body has been replaced with a Van Hool coach body.

Northern operated a shared service with Highland Omnibuses between Grantown and Elgin, so it was not uncommon to see a non-yellow bus operating within Northern territory. Here we see the afternoon departure from Elgin, with Highland's Willowbrook bodied Ford T74 returning to Grantown-on-Spey.

It was not usual for depots to use visiting coaches if they were operating on a private hire or tour, but if something unusual appeared as a result of a breakdown then it was fair game for use on local services. No doubt covering for a sick Ford that had been operating away from home, this Midland Duple Leopard MPE339 has been poached for a local run from Buckie to Cullen and is seen passing through Portknockie, being driven by James Hendry. (*James Mair*)

Midland's MPE339 had operated the coastal connecting service to Cullen, where passengers transferred to the direct Aberdeen-bound service, on this day being operated by Ford NT110. (*James Mair*)

Away Days and Long Distance

Northern operated a number of cross-Border express services in conjunction with Scottish Citylink and National Express. Various types of coaches were acquired for this purpose, some more successful than others. In the less successful category was the British-built MCW Metroliner single deck coach. Northern had two of the first style, NCM4 being the second. These were acquired for the 620-mile service to Plymouth.

The second batch of Metroliners had a more rounded appearance, but again suffered from reliability issues. In this view, NCM10 has been borrowed by Elgin depot for a hire to a Model Rail Show in Glasgow, but was being used on a local wedding hire the day before. No doubt Elgin-based driver Chris Hall appreciated the opportunity to drive something unusual.

Service 380 operated to Leeds and on this occasion NCT30 was the allocated coach. It is seen about to enter Dundee bus station.

As well as the Metroliner single deck coaches mentioned earlier, Northern operated three double deck Metroliners, mainly on the Aberdeen to London service. These were stunning looking vehicles at that time but their good looks disguised the same reliability issues that plagued the single deckers. Seen when new at a vintage vehicle show in Elgin is the third one of the trio, NDM12.

When Northern initially started the Aberdeen to London night service in 1974 they did not have appropriate vehicles within the fleet for such a quality service, so five Bristol RELH6G coaches were hired from Western SMT until appropriate coaches were acquired. Two of the five are seen at Aberdeen, DSD711D and DSD719D. As far as I know, fleet numbers were not allocated during their eight-month stay.

Acquired specifically for the overnight Aberdeen to London service, these Alexander M Type bodied Leopards certainly earned their keep. Six were acquired new for the 1975 season, NPE30 to NPE35, and were supplemented in the same year with two former identical coaches from Eastern Scottish, NPE 36 and NPE37, and one from Fife in 1979, allocated fleet number NPE76. NPE31 heads a three-coach convoy at London's Victoria Coach Station boarding passengers bound for Aberdeen.

These overnight coaches looked striking in their bright yellow and cream livery and with their reclining aircraft style seats, high performance saloon heaters supplemented with cosy travel rugs, and on board toilets were well suited to the arduous overnight motorway running they were designed for. NPE34 awaits its turn to board at Victoria Coach Station.

The yellow Northern livery was dropped in favour of the corporate Scottish saltire livery, applied to all express vehicles operated by the constituent companies of the Scottish Bus Group. As well as their London duties, the M Types would occasionally appear on hires or ad hoc and short notice work. Carrying a National Express label, NPE38, originally NPE76 when transferred from Fife, is seen at Keith Railway Station operating on rail replacement work. Rail passengers would have been transferred from the train for onward travel to either Aberdeen or Inverness. (*James Mair*)

To keep the overnight fleet up to date, six Duple Goldliner bodied Leyland Tigers were added to the fleet in 1982. Like the Alexander M Types they were replacing, they had small saloon windows suited for overnight travel. The second of the batch, NLT2, is seen departing Aberdeen bus station for London.

Northern secured the contract to transport Aberdeen Football Club to its various games around Scotland, and for that purpose one of the M Types, NPE76, was converted to a twenty-four-seat coach with tables. With Aberdeen FC being such a successful team at that time, a new executive coach was acquired specifically for team duties. A Duple bodied Leyland Tiger in full Scottish saltire livery arrived in 1982, carrying registration KSL41X and fleet number AFC1. The coach was subsequently reregistered 1412NE. With only twenty-eight seats and an onboard galley and microwave, this was considered luxury by those who had the privilege to travel on it. This view shows it in Aberdeen while parading with the team to celebrate the winning of more silverware.

Back to more mundane work again, and this time it is the annual outing for the Portgordon Pensioners group. My chariot for the day was NPE63, with NPE62 driven by Bill Pattinson. Here we have a short afternoon break at Glen Affric before heading back to Inverness for high tea.

This view was taken at Blackpool when NPE96 was new. I had taken a group of employees from the Baxter's factory in Fochabers to Blackpool for the illuminations weekend. Getting a new coach like this warranted the wearing of the best uniform, and I certainly felt king of the road heading down the M6 with such a fine coach.

Service 789 was a joint Buckie depot and Elgin depot service to Blackpool. Despite the weather, I can assure readers that this was a summer service! NPE98 was the coach allocated for this duty and it is seen heading for Buckie depot to uplift its contingent of passengers hoping to see some sunshine during their holiday.

For the 1983 season, a revised express livery was applied to a small number of coaches including NPE99, seen at Glasgow's Buchanan Street Bus Station. The original Duple seats had for some reason been replaced by seats from T Type Leopard NPE62. (*John Sinclair*)

Most of the rural depots were required to assist Aberdeen or, in some cases, Western and Central SMT with holiday duplication. This view was taken at Buckie on a Friday night prior to running light to Aberdeen. With a 2200 departure from Aberdeen, NPE102 would have travelled through the night to Blackpool, returning from Blackpool on the Saturday night with a load or sometimes empty.

A typical Blackpool scene on a summer Saturday afternoon with all the Northern drivers parking up together. On this particular trip we were all hired to Western SMT for the Glasgow Fair exodus to Blackpool. Having dropped off our passengers, we were awaiting instruction to return north.

Another local hire, this time for Buckie pensioners. NPE102, NT149 and NT76 are parked up at Banchory while our passengers amble into the town for their ice cream. NT149 was my allocation on that day, with NPE102 allocated to Jocky Morrison and NT76 allocated to George Pirie.

With no deckers allocated to Buckie, it was an unusual sight to see one travelling down the coast. NRD5 had been borrowed by Buckie depot for a church picnic outing from Findochty. The driver for that outing was George Pirie.

Buckie Thistle, known locally as The Jags, play in the Highland League and have over the years had reasonable cup success. The 1983 Highland League Cup final between The Jags and Keith was held at Borough Briggs, the home of Elgin City FC, and to cater for the large support attending the match four double deckers were hired by the local club. Here we see them await their passengers at Victoria Park before the short journey to Elgin. Unfortunately, Keith beat Buckie 1-0 on the day.

To add to the miscellany of coaches operated by Northern, two Leyland Royal Tiger Doyen coaches were acquired in 1984. They saw service on most cross-Border routes and were used on the occasional private hire as well as prestigious staff contract duties in Aberdeen for various oil companies. NRT20 is seen here outside the Aberdeen depot.

International hires have never featured greatly with Northern but this view shows that their coaches have been abroad. NRT20 is seen at the Zaan flour mill on an extended tour to the Dutch bulb fields.

Local and long distance tours have been operated by most Northern depots over the years. Aberdeen would have had the biggest tour itinerary and NT136 is typical of the tour coaches used for the 1976 summer programme.

My final selection for this chapter shows NT149 operating a day tour from Buckie to Ingliston Market near Edinburgh. Coach number one for the day was NPE45, driven by Bert Masson. Although the Leopard had better top speed than the Ford, I was able to catch up on the hills, where the Ford was able to hold a steady top speed.

Depots and Bus Stations

As well as displaying its fleet number, every Northern bus carried a plate indicating its home depot. From the early Alexander days through to around the late 1970s this would have been a cast metal plate, as shown in this photo. The plates were then replaced with transfers.

The parking area at Arbroath depot in 1982, showing withdrawn vehicles including former Tayside decker 153, which had been acquired for Tayway services but had been retired to Arbroath when this photo was taken.

This is where my interest and career started – the depot at East Cathcart Street, Buckie, telephone number 2266. The depot has long since been demolished, with a factory outlet shop built on the site.

A 1978 view of the Cumming Street bus station in Elgin prior to its closure and relocation to the rear of the High Street. Its closure was necessitated by the building of a new section of the A96, taking through traffic away from the city centre.

A night shot showing NPE63 about to depart for Huntly. This was the replacement bus station for the one at Cumming Street, but it too would be replaced during the construction of the St Giles shopping centre.

The stances at Elgin's relocated bus station when relatively new. Three platforms were used in service, the fourth being the parking bay for spare buses.

The Forres depot was acquired when Northern took over the Simpson's business in 1966. This view shows a typical mixed allocation as the depot was a sub depot of Elgin with no permanent allocations. (*John Sinclair*)

A lovely view of Macduff depot from one of the upper town streets. Since this photo was taken, the workshop and imposing office building have all been demolished. (*John Sinclair*)

The parking area at the old Guild Street bus station in Aberdeen.

Preserving the Name

The Bluebird emblem was first introduced by Alexander's in 1934, and today remains part of the trading name for the Stagecoach owned company that acquired the Northern Scottish operations.

A number of former Northern vehicles have been saved by preservationists, testament to the engineering staff employed by the company over the years. Having spent more time in preservation than in actual service, NPA44 has been a regular attendee at rallies up and down the country since withdrawal from service in 1971. I travelled to school on this bus many a time and was pleased to see it paying a visit to its old depot during July 1980.

My first efforts at preservation involved NPA181, a 1947 Leyland Tiger PS1 new in 1950. The cost for the body when new was £1,580. When withdrawn from service, it was sold to Ross Poultry in Aberdeen for staff transport. I acquired it in 1977 for the sum of £100, but the work required to bring it back to original condition was beyond my means. While in my ownership it was kept at Kinloss, sharing yard space with NPC25.

NPA181 has now been fully restored and resides at the Scottish Vintage Bus Museum. It returned north in 2006, travelling along the routes it served for many years. For the journey from Inverness to Macduff, NPA181 was accompanied by preserved NPE102, and both my father and I enjoyed our reunion with this former Buckie bus. Here it is seen in Portknockie during that trip.

I mentioned earlier my interest in NPE102. When withdrawn by Stagecoach, I and a number of colleagues acquired the vehicle and had it restored to its original external condition. We rallied it at various locations throughout the UK, including Showbus at Duxford. It is now owned by members of the Angus Transport group. It is seen in Banff Low Street soon after restoration.

To mark the fiftieth anniversary of the Northern company, Stagecoach repainted one of their Plaxton Profile bodied Volvo B7R coaches into the original yellow livery, in a manner that mirrored the livery application on the M Type London coaches. Elgin allocated 53334 is seen at Cullen being driven by Gordon Pirie, a driver who was based at Elgin when the original Northern and Northern Scottish companies were operating.

As a reminder of the past, models representing the Northern company have been produced, including single and double decker models. The latest release is a small-scale replica of the Burlingham Sun Saloon. Hopefully, further examples of Northern and Northern Scottish buses will be produced in the future.